Capricorn

21 December – 20 January

amber
BOOKS

ASTROLOGICAL SIGN DATES:
The precise start and end times for each sign vary by a day or two from year to year as the Gregorian calendar shifts relative to the tropical year. The dates provided in this book are correct for the year 2020.

If you are unsure of the Zodiac sign for your specific birth year, visit: www.yourzodiacsign.com.

Capricorn

21 December – 20 January

A guide to understanding yourself, your friendships and finding your true love

This edition first published in 2020 by
Amber Books Ltd
United House
North Road
London N7 9DP
United Kingdom
www.amberbooks.co.uk
Instagram: amberbooksltd
Facebook: amberbooks
Twitter: @amberbooks

ISBN: 978-1-83886-029-5

Project Editor: Sarah Uttridge
Design: Zoë Mellors

Picture Credits:
All illustrations by Fabbri Publications except the following:
Shutterstock: 30, (PODIS), 32 (La Puma), 35 (Slonomysh), 40 (Angel Soler Gollonet)

Printed and bound in China

TRADITIONAL CHINESE BOOKBINDING
This book has been produced using traditional Chinese bookbinding techniques, using a method that was developed during the Ming Dynasty (1368–1644) and remained in use until the adoption of Western binding techniques in the early 1900s. In traditional Chinese binding, single sheets of paper are printed on one side only, and each sheet is folded in half, with the printed pages on the outside. The book block is then sandwiched between two boards and sewn together through punched holes close to the cut edges of the folded sheets.

Contents

Introduction

Capricorn

21 December–20 January

Sign: The Goat
Ruling Planet: Saturn
Gender: Feminine
Element: Earth
Quality: Cardinal
Compatibility: Taurus and Virgo
Non-compatibility: Sagittarius and Aries

Every man, woman and child is born with a distinct and different destiny. There are no exceptions. Everyone has cosmic significance and a part to play in the life of the universe. This is innate and inescapable, and goes beyond the tiny boundaries of nation, creed and colour.

As we live out our lives on planet Earth, we are, however unknowingly, acting in a greater drama and reacting to impulses that come from distant astronomical bodies, stars and planets millions of light years away. Sceptics pour scorn on the idea that far-distant Saturn, for example, can have any effect on our lives, as the ancient art and science of astrology teaches. But the fact is that we are sparks of energy inhabiting bodies made of the same stuff as the stars, responding like tiny radios to the distant messages they send to Earth.

Each infant carries within it a double blueprint for life: its genetic programming and the pattern of character that comes from the astrological 'clock' that was set in motion at the moment of birth. No one knows the full extent of genetic influence, although it seems to be astonishingly far-reaching, but the power of the horoscope has been well known to the wisest men and women for many centuries.

Our Sun signs provide essential inside information about our destinies. They reveal the secrets of who we really are, and why we are here, laying out before us our potential, the sort of joys and achievements our characteristics may bring about, and warn us of problems to be overcome through the triumph of free will.

Read this book with an open mind and discover who you really are.

The Elements

Up to the beginning of the Age of Enlightenment – the modern scientific era – in the 18th century, it was commonly believed that everything, including human beings, was made up of the four elements: Earth, Air, Fire and Water. These were thought of as the building blocks of life, and each astrological sign had a predominance of one or another. Each created its common characteristics, although too much of any of the elements can produce an unbalanced personality.

Earth Signs

Those signs ruled by Earth are Taurus, Virgo and Capricorn. Each manifests the element in different ways. However, in all cases, Earth makes those born under these signs tend to be more practical, sensible and stable than most. They are better 'grounded' or, to put it in another way, they keep their feet on the ground. Whereas others may rush off on madcap schemes or sit around and daydream, those born under Earth signs roll up their sleeves and quietly get on with the job. For example, Arians may be the great explorers and adventurers of the zodiac, but it is Taureans who follow behind, set up camp for them and arrange for provisions to be sent ahead upriver. Taureans are 'the salt of the earth', the plodders who may strike the more dynamic and extrovert signs of the zodiac as being uninspired, but who are invaluable and upright members of society.

Virgoans, always organized, tidy and efficient, are the analysts and notekeepers who keep track of records, accounts and archives so that society knows its history. They are the ones who ensure that the great exploits of the Arian adventurers are known to posterity. Capricornians always have an eye to the future, planning ahead for a rainy day from their lofty mountain peaks, like the Goat that symbolizes their sign. And if they are occasionally dour and pessimistic – thanks to the influence of their ruling planet Saturn, who nevertheless encourages them to be disciplined and careful – then they succeed all the more in keeping the wilder excesses of the Fire and Air signs under control.

Earth Signs
Taurus
Virgo
Capricorn

Colours of the Zodiac

Traditionally, each sign of the zodiac has its own colour, which is believed to be 'lucky' or magically empowered for those born under that particular sign. In general, the colours are associated with the ruling planets and are symbolic of their attributes. Many people find that they feel most comfortable when wearing their sign's colours, and often choose them without knowing their full astrological background.

Capricorn

Ruling Planet: Saturn.

Colours: Dark brown, black and grey.

Introspective and wintry, those born under the sign of the Goat need to escape from, rather than use, their sign's traditional colours or at least cheer themselves up with brighter, more positive and outgoing colours such as pink, yellow or red.

The Angelic Hierarchy

According to ancient tradition, each planet is governed by one of the great archangels, who also rule aspects of human life. The box below lists the planet that they govern, the areas they influence and their day of the week.

Cassiel

Archangel of Saturn.

Governs: Capricorn.

Rules: Property, land and legacies, the elderly, the Eastern belief of ultimate justice through rebirth, karma, and the fate of humanity.

Day: Saturday.

The Genders

Traditionally, the twelve signs of the zodiac are divided into Masculine and Feminine, although of course both men and women are born into each.

The characteristics were assigned to the genders aeons ago, well before modern feminism or political correctness, and may now seem old-fashioned to many. However, the signs do seem to be grouped according to the appropriate gender.

The Feminine Signs

The Feminine signs are Taurus, Cancer, Virgo, Scorpio, Capricorn and Pisces. Feminine traits tend to be accentuated most in the Water signs of Cancer and Pisces.

These signs present gentler, more passive qualities. They are the carers and the nurturers, inclined to take a back seat and worry over the well-being of others. They are artistic and in tune with their intuition, and may be psychic. Self-evidently, these are the motherly and sisterly signs, with all the attendant positive and negative characteristics. They tend to be the power behind the throne, rather than movers and shakers, although many are great achievers, especially in the modern, more egalitarian world, where their qualities are encouraged.

Negatively, the Feminine signs can be fussy, possessive, mean-minded, vindictive, cringing, clinging and over-emotional.

Aquarius, the sign of the coming Age, is endowed with both Masculine and Feminine traits, although it is traditionally categorized as Masculine.

The Ruling Planets

Until the 18th century, astrologers knew only the planets of our solar system that could be seen with the naked eye: Mercury, Venus, Mars, Jupiter and Saturn. (For the purposes of astrology, the Sun and the Moon are also counted as planets even though the Sun is a star and the Moon is the satellite of Earth.) Uranus was discovered in 1781, Neptune in 1846 and Pluto was first seen in 1930. Many astrologers believe that the existence of other heavenly bodies – such as the rumoured Vulcan, which hypothetically exists within the orbit of Mercury – is about to be confirmed. Astrologers will then have to agree which signs these 'new' planets will rule, and what human characteristics their discovery will accentuate.

Saturn

The god Saturn originally governed the agricultural arts and skills, but later he gave his name to one of Rome's favourite festivals – Saturnalia, in which the dark of winter was enlivened with music, dancing and feasting. This usually took place at the winter solstice of 20–21 December, although when the Christians took over and sanitized the feast day of Saturnalia, it was moved to 25 December to encompass other pagan festivals, including the celebration of the birth of gods such as Dionysus.

Because Saturn was once thought to lie at the remote edge of the solar system, it has come to represent coldness, distance and limitation. Many of the old astrologers were repelled and frightened by Saturn, a view reflected in the adjective 'saturnine' – meaning gloomy, taciturn and somewhat sinister. However, we now know that Saturn does not mark the edge of the planetary system, and astrologers no longer consider it to be totally negative in its influence on humankind.

Saturn rules Capricorn (and, more controversially, Aquarius), bestowing the mixed blessing of great karmic lessons on those born under the sign of the

About Saturn

At 120,000 km (74,600 miles) in diameter, Saturn is the second-largest planet in our solar system. It is 1427 million km (887 million miles) away from the Sun, which it takes 29 years to orbit. The largest of its 12 moons is Titan. Saturn is surrounded by many hundreds of rings, which are composed of chunks of rock and ice.

The day sacred to Saturn is, of course, Saturday.

Goat. It can bring restrictions in its wake, and can make its subjects inclined to be narrow in outlook. However, it is also the bringer of tenacity and the wisdom that comes from learning the hard way.

The Qualities

In addition to the influence of gender, the elements and the planets, each sign of the zodiac is affected by having an intrinsic quality – Cardinal, Fixed or Mutable.

Cardinal Quality

Those with a strong Cardinal quality to their chart are, traditionally, supremely ambitious and perhaps somewhat ruthless in getting to the top. They are bursting with ideas and are dynamic in pursuing their goals, especially where their careers are concerned. They see themselves as achievers and winners: every day is a challenge that they willingly accept. Their sense of determination inspires others, although they themselves will continue to take the lead and initiate every new project. They can be dismissive of lesser mortals. Cardinality also represents new beginnings.

Capricorn

Like the Goat of their sign, Capricornians will react with fury if anyone attempts to domineer them. There will come a point when they erupt, put their heads down – and charge! They also harbour strong, long-term ambitions, which they determinedly pursue, even though it may take them years to achieve them. Many Capricornians are not happy in a competitive situation and will do anything to end it – but only by winning.

Signs and Symbols

Most people are familiar with the zodiac 'zoo' – the collection of symbols that represent the twelve signs. These images reflect the characteristics traditionally assigned to each sign and contain a wealth of knowledge about its true nature.

Each sign of the zodiac is represented by a symbol – the twin fish for Pisces, for example. No one is sure exactly when or why the symbols were chosen, although some authorities believe they date from Sumeria or Mesopotamia, 4000 years before Jesus Christ. The priest-astrologers of the ancient world were the first to impose recognizable patterns on the great constellations – Leo the Lion being one example.

Today, seeing such shapes in the stars may seem fanciful, but thousands of years ago imaginations were more poetic, and many myths told of magical animals, such as the dragon, which had strange powers to influence everyday human life.

Although the ancient Egyptians left few astrological records, they were almost unique in antiquity for worshipping archetypal, animal-headed gods. However, these strange hybrid gods – half-human, half-animal – were worshipped as aspects of one God. Contrary to the general belief that the Egyptians were idolaters, their religion was basically monotheistic. Each statue represented an aspect of the one true God.

Since they were established, the signs have remained unchanged, although there was a movement in the Middle Ages to change the sign of Aquarius to the sign of John the Baptist – presumably because of the connection with water.

The twelve signs of the zodiac do seem particularly apt on the whole, and accurately reflect the archetypal character of Sun sign types. The great Swiss psychoanalyst Carl Gustav Jung (1875–1961) believed that, deep in our psyches, humanity shares a collective unconscious – a set of archetypal images, which, at a profound level, we all understand. The signs of the zodiac form part of this pool of images, conveying eternal truths to our unconscious minds.

Signs and Symbols

Capricorn The Goat

The goat is a highly adaptive creature who can – and often does – eat just about anything. It can also live just about anywhere, even in some very hostile environments.

The goat is usually a pleasant, amenable beast, getting on well with its own kind, other animals and humans alike, and producing delightful milk. However, goats can be difficult, as any farmer who keeps them will attest. They can also be very destructive. Goats frequently appear to come

from nowhere to land a very painful butt on the particularly tender areas of humans.

In Christian countries, the goat has had a bad reputation as an associate of the Devil. During the witchcraft hysteria that began in 15th-century Europe, it was believed that witches flew on their broomsticks to unholy Sabbats, or meetings with the Devil, in which their evil master appeared as a gigantic goat. This was said to represent the worship of the Goat of Mendes (or Memphis) in ancient Egypt, for which there is little or no evidence. Later, this idea was amended: the Satanist High Priest was said to wear a mask of the Goat of Mendes while presiding over filthy – that is, sexual – rites in his master's name. Modern researchers have found no evidence that such ceremonies ever took place.

The Sun in Capricorn

Sun sign Capricornians are disciplined, methodical, sensible and sensitive. If that makes them sound cold and boring, the truth is that they can be, but often they show remarkable ambition, kindness and gentle, often self-deprecating, humour. Traditionally, their ruling planet Saturn is concerned with the tough lessons of life: illness, restriction, old age and death, but modern astrologers realize that this picture is far too gloomy. While Saturn can be a tough teacher, often repeatedly putting Capricornians through a steep learning curve, it can also galvanize them into action, to get things done, become achievers and climb to the top of their chosen profession with all its attendant status and prosperity.

Capricornians tend to be cautious by nature, sensing pitfalls and obstacles and standing back from problems. This can make them pessimistic and disinclined to move forward: inside they are saying to themselves, not 'you might fail', but 'you will fail'. Some can become so convinced that nothing good will ever happen that their unconscious mind ensures that nothing does. However, the whole point of the Saturnine influence is to present them with a series of challenges that will never actually be too difficult for them to overcome – for those who believe in karma, this is actually an honour. Once Capricornians have come to understand the true nature of their path, it will be easier for them to rise above the mundane pettiness and worries that often beset them.

Sticklers for detail, and methodical to a fault, Capricornians are superb organizers, happy to deal

Personality Traits of Capricornians

Positive:	*Negative:*
Disciplined	Cautious
Methodical	Pessimistic
Sensible	Inflexible
Sensitive	Fussy
Ambitious	Plodders
Gentle	Unforgiving
Hard-working	

with paperwork and the daily business of life. They are not natural stars like Leos or Scorpians, but usually seek to oil the wheels behind the scenes and make everything run smoothly. They hate untidiness, dirt and mess, whether it is the house or is expressed as a state of mind. Of course, many more sloppy characters consider them irritating and fussy. They can seem joyless and obsessed with doing the right thing, being conventional and often reactionary, with rigid, inflexible, self-imposed rules. But when they let go and relax – even with Saturn as a ruler, this is not impossible! – they are charming, delightful companions, with a wonderfully dry sense of humour.

Appearance

Many typical Sun sign Capricornians especially the men – look rather goatish, with prominent noses and angular features. They tend to be on the tall side and somewhat bony, with dark, straight hair. The women are often of medium height, with mousey hair and strong features, although they can have beautiful, serene expressions that give them an attractive air.

Capricornians of both sexes take great care with their appearance, but hate any form of flamboyance, extravagance or eccentricity. They are neat, clean and perhaps slightly old-fashioned. Capricornian females are true ladies – a term that pleases them. They like to have their hair beautifully styled and regularly tinted in subtle, natural-looking colours. Even young Capricornian females are wary of the latest high street trends and tend to stick with the more tried and tested styles. Capricornian men love collars, ties and formal suits. Their wardrobes usually lack casual T-shirts and jeans, and even if they wear them, they look completely wrong.

Health

Capricornians think it bad form to admit to illness, and often force themselves to crawl to work even when they are suffering from really debilitating viruses. They hate what they see as weakness, and continually berate themselves for

feeling off-colour. This attitude can result in serious problems going untreated – they despise people who 'bother' doctors – often making the situation much worse. Their tendency to bottle up emotions can also result in health problems in later life. Research has shown that people who express their anger, disappointment and grief are much more likely to avoid illnesses such as heart attacks – and even some forms of cancer – than those who do not let them out.

Traditionally, Capricornian problem areas are their joints, bones and teeth. There is a tendency to stiffness and arthritis, although it can be relatively mild. They need to take extra calcium, cod liver oil and evening primrose oil supplements to help their physical flexibility. They should move around more, disciplining themselves to have regular breaks, especially if working long hours at a computer, because they have a tendency to Repetitive Strain Injury (RSI). Although they are inclined to take only conventional medicine seriously, they should at least try complementary therapies. Acupressure and aromatherapy will help to loosen them up, both physically and emotionally. They should have regular sessions with an osteopath or chiropractor and be sure to visit the dentist regularly.

Career

Sun sign Capricornians are highly industrious and formidably organized, so they make superb administrators. They are happy to sit alone at their desk all day, taking, and often giving, orders by telephone, memo or in curiously formal emails. There is a certain haughtiness about them, a detached air that sets them apart from their chattier, more relaxed colleagues and can make them seem intimidating and aloof. However, they have no wish to be seen as one of the crowd. They frequently have their eye on the top job, and are content to work their way towards it in gradual stages. Aiming too high and too soon is likely to be disastrous for a typical Sun sign Capricornian, although they are unlikely to try it more than once. One bad mistake in business or career, and Capricornians have learned a lesson for life.

Traditionally associated with the Earth, Capricornians are attracted to gardening and environmental issues, and can make stalwart supporters of 'green' campaigns, either as a full-time job or a part-time interest.

Rather austere and unimaginative, they make excellent bank employees, although they are perhaps more suited to the old Dickensian days of wing collars and great dusty ledgers than today's relaxed style of 'personal bankers' and online transactions. They are often career civil servants, rising gradually through the grades to a very high position of respect and authority. Sun sign Capricornians are very good with money matters and are scrupulously honest, which makes them ideal in positions of trust.

Their self-discipline and methodical working style mean that they are happy to tackle the painstaking

The best careers for Capricornians

- Office manager
- Environmentalist
- Banker
- Tax inspector
- Customs officer
- Gardener
- Civil servant

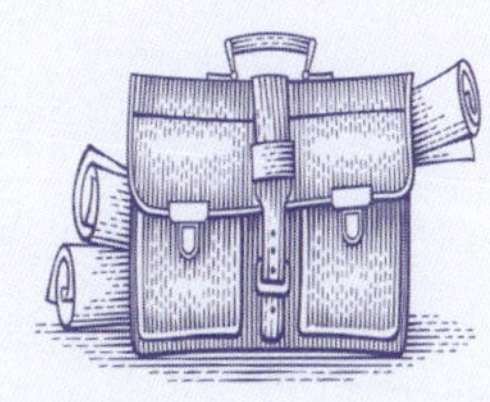

jobs that others avoid, and they may even choose unpopular careers – as tax inspectors or customs officers, for example. They see duty and law enforcement as of paramount importance, and can become overbearing, perhaps even sadistic with lesser mortals who owe tax or are not familiar with rules and regulations. Most Capricornians, however, have a kind streak, and become very hurt at the idea that they might abuse their position of power.

Capricornians tend to have very low self-worth, and see their work as a reflection of the respect they have earned. They love to be pillars of the community, and often take on time-consuming local council work, or help out in charity shops besides having a full-time job.

Redundancy hits them harder than any other Sun sign: they take it very personally, seeing 'the sack' as their own failure, and feel they will never find another job or make their mark in life. Unemployment is always a bleak experience, but to Capricornians it represents the winter of all their hopes. Of course, many do dust themselves down and successfully start all over again, but the threat of being unemployed haunts the typical Capricornian like a curse waiting to fall on them.

Relationships

Capricornians can be surprisingly passionate behind closed doors – after all, theirs is the sign of the Goat! However, they take a while to warm up, are very cautious about relating to others, and tend to be 'backward in coming forward'. Many Capricornians of both sexes can wait an unfashionably long time before losing their virginity and can be very timid with the opposite sex.

Capricornians are very rarely easy-going and can, in fact, be rather dour. They need to be encouraged to lighten up. They can be over-keen on pouring cold water on the bright ideas of more enthusiastic family members. Their ultimate accolade is more likely to be 'That's quite good' instead of heartfelt congratulations – an approach that can be discouraging, especially to young children.

Capricornians often marry relatively late in life, waiting until they can afford a comfortable home in an upmarket area. They will spend weeks peering into estate agents' windows and making calculations about how much they can afford, without ever thinking that a house must be a home and have love, as well as money, lavished on it.

Some Capricornians are constantly worried about money, scrimping and saving even though they earn a

decent salary. To them, destitution is only around the corner, and Fate will hand them a place on Skid Row unless they are vigilant and count the pennies every moment of their lives. This is a manifestation of their low self-esteem: the more money they salt away, the more respectable they are in their own eyes.

Capricornians need to learn to relax and feel secure in their homes, without any threat to the status quo. They are very unhappy with emotional scenes and upheaval. They tend to carry their early hurt around with them like ice in their hearts, although they can thaw out if their partner loves them determinedly and wholeheartedly, gradually introducing them to the concept of receiving love and all good things. They must learn to accept that they are worthy of the devotion of others.

Many Capricornians tend to stoicism and reserve, believing that dignity must be maintained at all costs, even in front of their nearest and dearest. Although this can be good for their family, who see them as towers of strength in a crisis, it is less useful for their own health. Capricornians can bottle up a huge backlog of grief and anger, often giving the appearance of cold-heartedness at the death of relatives, even of a spouse or parent. They can take refuge behind clichés such as 'Life must go on' and 'Crying won't bring them back', but inside they are bleeding. Family members should try to encourage Capricornians to discuss their feelings, whether those are of grief or joy.

Capricorns always try to do the right thing in life, and cannot understand those who rebel against the system, so they hardly make ideal parents of boisterous children or difficult teenagers. But they will always be proud (in a quiet, unassuming way) of their more timid, studious and sensible offspring.

Ideal Partner

Capricornians need a strong, loving partner who neither whines nor clings, causes scenes or is too adventurous. Intense, dreamy Pisceans rarely fit the bill, and fellow Water sign Cancerians are usually far too emotionally demanding. Earthy Taureans and Virgoans, who have a similar fondness for order and neatness, but possess added charm and wit, possibly make the best partners for the wintry Capricornians. It would be a mistake for a typical Goat even to consider a relationship with a happy-go-lucky Sagittarian or a wild-child Arian. Opposites may attract, but they can often destroy, too.

Compatibility in Relationships

Aries
20 March–19 April

Fiery, tempestuous Arians may be appealingly different, but this opposite sign will be too cold to attract for long.

Capricorn
21 December–20 January

Two wintry Goats together may not make for much empathizing, but sometimes like works with like.

Cancer
21 June–21 July

Cancerian emotion can drive Capricornians mad, although their compassion and loving home have certain attractions.

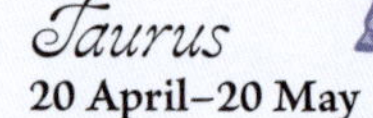

Taurus
20 April–20 May

Earthy and controlled Taureans have a lot to offer the Goat, and they can bring out the passion in each other.

Libra
23 September–22 October

Librans' love of the social whirl can cause problems for the more withdrawn and hesitant type of Capricornian.

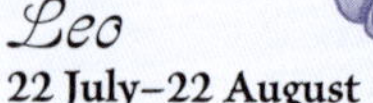

Leo
22 July–22 August

Capricornians admire Leonine style and dash, but are fearful of such high-profile egocentrics.

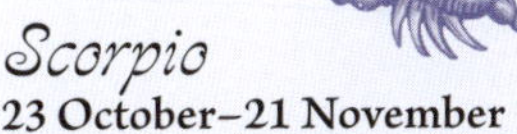

Scorpio

23 October–21 November

Intrigued by fascinating Scorpio, Capricorn may make a serious error of judgement – and live to regret it.

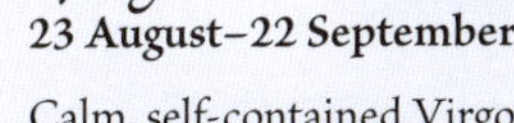

Virgo

23 August–22 September

Calm, self-contained Virgoans often make excellent partners for cautious, conventional Capricornians.

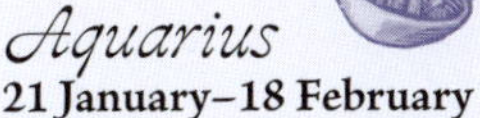

Aquarius

21 January–18 February

This combination can work, if only because Aquarians can get on with most people if they are prepared to compromise.

Sagittarius

22 November–20 December

Unfettered by practicalities, Sagittarians seriously upset Capricornian respect for the more traditional way of life.

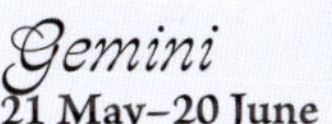

Gemini

21 May–20 June

Gregarious, persuasive Geminians can charm reserved Capricornians, but the Goat remains distrustful.

Pisces

19 February–19 March

Contradictory and often unhappy Pisceans will bewilder Capricornians, who are scared by overt emotion.

The Capricornian Child

Capricornians are rarely happy children. Even if their parents love them to distraction, the constant fear of losing their father or mother will seriously detract from their happiness. Capricornians are frequently far too fearful and sad, needing endless encouragement to join in the fun, get their hands dirty and have a laugh. Although naturally self-disciplined, they look to their elders and betters to give them clear ground rules for their behaviour, and can be soon become very distressed in an easy-going, irresponsible atmosphere.

Capricornian children need to be given responsibility at an early age so that they can feel they are making a contribution. They should be praised at every opportunity in order to bolster their underdeveloped self-esteem. This is quite safe, because there is no danger of Capricornians ever becoming conceited.

Sun sign Capricornians are always old, even when young children. It is as if they carry all the problems of the world on their tiny shoulders, and they can become very introverted. They should never be bullied or teased, but always gently encouraged to make their contribution, and to make steady, rather than spectacular, success at school. It is also important that they are never compared unfavourably with any of their siblings or the flashy, natural-born achievers in their class. What they like to hear is that everything comes to those who wait.

Famous Capricorns

David Bowie

Louis Braille

Charles Rennie Mackintosh

Muhammad Ali

Simone de Beauvoir

Bernadette, Saint of Lourdes

Al Capone

Paul Cézanne

Marlene Dietrich

Oliver Hardy

Martin Luther King

J. Edgar Hoover

Joan of Arc

Mao Tse Tung

Isaac Newton

Michel de Nostradamus

Louis Pasteur

Edgar Allen Poe

Elvis Presley

Henri Matisse

Finding Your Sun Sign (2020 dates)

Aries	20 March–19 April*
Taurus	20 April–20 May
Gemini	21 May–20 June
Cancer	21 June–21 July
Leo	22 July–22 August
Virgo	23 August–22 September
Libra	23 September–22 October
Scorpio	23 October–21 November
Sagittarius	22 November–20 December
Capricorn	21 December–20 January
Aquarius	21 January–18 February
Pisces	19 February–19 March

*The dates provided in this book reflect the year 2020. Dates may vary by a day or two from year to year.